Eschatology Unlimited

Dennis Mather

WESTBOW
PRESS®
A DIVISION OF THOMAS NELSON
& ZONDERVAN

WestBow Press books may be ordered through booksellers or by contacting:

WestBow Press
A Division of Thomas Nelson & Zondervan
1663 Liberty Drive
Bloomington, IN 47403
www.westbowpress.com
1 (866) 928-1240

ISBN: 978-1-9736-1694-8 (sc)
ISBN: 978-1-9736-1693-1 (e)

Print information available on the last page.

WestBow Press rev. date: 1/31/2018

Preface

The theology that pertains to things that happen in the last days is quite often called 'prophecy', but the technical term is 'eschatology'.

In the Old Testament prophecy was "predictions", but now in this day and age it is, "speaking forth the written Scripture".[1] This is because we now have the completed Word of God in our present canon of scripture, and we need no further predictions pertaining to the last days. Scripture just needs to be diligently studied, so that the Holy Spirit can illuminate it for you.

The next thing that's going to happen in history is our "Blessed Hope", or the rapture (Titus 2:13; 1 Thessalonians 4:14-18). It is my favorite part of the doctrine of last things, because I'm going to participate in it!

---

[1] James Strong says in his dictionary, *The Exhaustive Concordance of the Bible* (New York and Nashville: Abingdon Press), (item #4396) that a prophet is someone "who has insight into divine things and speaks them forth to others." This refers to our modern day preachers who expound the Scriptures in such a manner that people are compelled to hear.

CHAPTER ONE

A Systematic Theology of Eschatology

Eschatology is the Greek words 'eschatos'[2] and 'ology' put together. Eschatos means "latter end" and speaks of those things that will be happening at the end of, and directly after, our present dispensation.[3]

And "ology" means "science" in Greek.

We do not know exactly when these events will take place, because "it is not for you to know" (Acts 1:7 in the NKJV). However, we can know the general time frame (Lu.

---

[2]   Ibid., (item #2078).

[3]   A dispensation is a dispensing of God's grace that takes place in a time period. This grace is different in each period of time, so that what constituted a salvation plan in the previous dispensation is invalid in the present dispensation. This is due to progressive revelation. For instance, the Patriarch dispensation didn't have the Ten Commandments and the Mosaic dispensation didn't have the Immanuel coming of Jesus Christ.

     There have been six dispensations put into effect since the fall of man. They are: 1.) Conscience; 2.) Human Government; 3.) Patriarch; 4.) Mosaic; 5.) Kingship; and 6.) the Church. The Millennium, which is the seventh dispensation, is still in the future.

21:29-31), and one of the best ways of knowing this is the fact that Israel is being regathered (Ezek. 36:24 ; Ezek. 37; Zeph. 3:14-20; Zech. 10:8-11; Rom. 9:15,16). She is getting ready for having her Messiah sitting on David's throne in Jerusalem during the Millennium. This is happening, even though Israel is now in a state of unbelief.

On top of this, the 'gathering around Jerusalem for battle' (Zech 14:2; Rev. 16:16; 19:19) that is spoken of in the Bible is beginning. This is because of the hatred of many people for the Jewish state, especially those in her immediate vicinity.

We will examine these things and seven others in this treatise. They are: 1.) the apostasy; 2.) the rapture; 3.) the tribulation period; 4.) the glorious second coming of Jesus Christ; 5.) the resurrections and judgments; 6.) the millennium; and 7.) the new Heaven and new earth.

I. The Apostasy:

The apostasy is where we are living right now and is based upon the fact that "the mystery of lawlessness is already at work" (2 Thess. 2:7 in the NKJV). The stage is being set for those things that are going to happen right after our present dispensation ends. So it is good to know what is going on in our present day.

Many things are included in this apostasy. Three of these are: 1.), mankind is now in a condition that is commensurate with that which is depicted in 2 Timothy chapter three, verses 1-7. It is speaking of gross immorality; 2.) there is an increase of knowledge in the latter days predicted by Daniel in Daniel chapter 12, verse 4; and 3.) the world can only think of one thing, and that is the quest to become a one-world society.

So it can be seen by these facts that we are in the last days just prior to the rapture of the Church (Matt. 24:32,33,37-41; 2 Thess. 2:7,8).

II. The Rapture:

The rapture is when born again Christians of all nations will be delivered from "the wrath to come" (1 Thess. 1:10 in the NKJV; and the concept of the rapture in Rev. 3:10). It is the event that will end the church dispensation and is the next event in eschatological history.

It is accomplished by our being caught up into the clouds to be with Jesus Christ (1 Cor. 15:51-54; 1 Thess. 4:14-18) and is certainly our "blessed hope" (Ti. 2:13 in the NKJV). It is also why everyone who is born again is at the 'marriage' and the 'marriage supper' of the Lamb in Heaven (2 Cor. 5:8; Rev. 19:7,9) while everyone who did not participate in it is left on earth to go through the Great Tribulation.

III. The Great Tribulation:

The Tribulation is that period of time between the rapture and the glorious second coming of Jesus Christ. It takes place on earth while born again believers are in heaven.[4] It has also been known as Daniel's seventieth week (Dan. 9:24-27),[5] the time of 'Jacob's trouble' (Jer. 30:4-9), and "the hour of trial" for the gentiles (Rev. 3:10 in the NKJV).

The tribulation period is seven years in length and has two halves, each three and one-half years long (Dan. 9:27). The first half sees the regimes of the anti-Christ and the false prophet come into being,[6] and only during this time in history will the world see these two in power (2 Thess. 2:7,8; Rev. 6:2-11). The second half is very cataclysmic and is the judgment of the gentiles (2 Thess. 2:9-12; Rev. 6:12-17).

---

[4] We are in Heaven only for a short time, because Revelation 19:14 says we will be coming back with Jesus when He returns. We go to Heaven to sleep when we die (1 Cor. 15:20; 1 Thess. 4.14,15), and when we awake we are to have a huge wedding and a great banquet (Rev. 19:7-9). This is before we saddle up on white horses behind Him when he is ready to return. Those who are raptured go to the wedding and banquet without sleeping (1 Cor. 15:51, however, this is after a great welcoming ceremony.

[5] Daniel's seventieth week is based upon the weeks in Daniel, chapter nine, verses 24 to 27. They are seven year periods, and it will be seen that the Church dispensation is a parenthesis inside the Kingship dispensation between Daniel's 62nd and 69th weeks (Dan 9:24-27). Our dispensation was put into affect so that the Gentiles could come to know the Messiah. It is portrayed for us in Romans 9:24-11:15.

[6] The anti-Christ will someday be the dictator of the world (Rev. 13:1-10; Dan. 11:21-45; Rev. 17:7,8,11), and the False Prophet will someday be the leader of the "one world church" (Rev. 13:11-18; 17:1b-6,9,18; 18:2-24).

Israel has somewhat peaceful conditions in the first half of the tribulation, because she has entered into a peace pact with the anti-Christ (Dan. 11:21-23; Isa. 28:14-18) through the help of the false prophet (Rev. 13:12; Zech. 11:16,17; Rev. 18:3). But even this treaty does not insure a lasting peace for Israel, because at the half-way mark of the Tribulation the anti-Christ and the false prophet desecrate the temple that has been built in Jerusalem (Dan. 11:31; Matt. 24:15). This is when a devout remnant of Israel flees to a safe place (Matt. 24:16-20; Mk. 13:14-20; Lk. 21:20,21; Rev. 12:6,14-16) that has been prepared for her in the countries of Edom, Moab, and Ammon (Dan. 11:41; Rev. 12:16a).[7]

The second half of the tribulation is when our Lord judges the earth. Much is said in the Bible about this (Zech. 14:1-6; Rev. 6:12-17; 8:7-21; 14:18-20; 16:1-21; 19:17-21), because God does not wish that anybody should have to go through it (2 Pet. 3:9). The first half of the Tribulation may bring wars, famines, diseases, and a dictator (Rev. 6:1-9), but the

---

[7] In *The Wycliffe Bible Commentary,* (The Moody Bible Institute-1962), Wilbur Smith says while commenting on Revelation 12:13-17 that "the earth's aiding the woman (v. 16) may represent, as Walter Scott says, 'the governments of the earth befriending the Jew and providentially (how, we know not) frustrating the efforts of the serpent.'" So the countries south and east of Israel (Edom, Moab, and Ammon) are ancient Arabic countries that were in the general area that is now the country of Saudi Arabia. They will again aid Israel in the future when she is under persecution. They did this unknowingly in 1991 during the Persian Gulf War when it was thought that the leader of Iraq, Saddam Hussein, had for one of his goals the destruction of Israel. Saudi Arabia hosted the armies that ousted Saddam.

second half brings cataclysmic devastation that is such as mankind has never seen before (Dan. 12:1b; Rev. 6:12-17). That this period of time is very short is indicative of the fact that God is very merciful (Matt. 24:22; Mk. 13:19,20).

IV. The Glorious Return of Jesus Christ:

The glorious return of Jesus Christ is also known as the second coming of Jesus Christ because it is the second time He actually puts His feet on the ground.[8] It occurs at the end of the tribulation period and is for the purpose of curtailing the activities of both the anti-Christ and the false-prophet who have gathered the entire world together for battle against Israel.

Jesus comes quickly, as He said He would (Rev. 3:11; 22:7,12,20), and the anti-Christ and the false-prophet are put directly into "the lake of fire burning with brimstone" (Rev. 19:20 in the NKJV).

Everyone else who is present at this battle known as Armageddon is "slain with the sword of Him that sat upon the horse, which sword proceeded out of His mouth" (Rev. 19:21 in the KJV). And the person sitting on the horse is Jesus Christ at His second coming.

---

[8] At the Rapture Jesus catches us up into the clouds (1 Thess. 4:17), but at the Second Coming He comes down through the clouds and puts His feet on the ground (Matt. 24:30; 26:64; Dan 7:13; Lk. 21:27; Mk. 13:26; 14:62). And it is putting His feet on the ground that constitutes an advent.

V. The Resurrections and Judgments:

There are three resurrections in the future that are all in conjunction with three judgments (Heb. 9:27). They are: 1.) one that pertains to born again Christians; 2.) one that pertains to righteous Old Testament saints; and 3.) one that is for the unsaved of all ages.

A. The Resurrection and Judgment for Christians:

The resurrection we are speaking of for Christians is the rapture (1Thess. 4:17), and the judgment is the "judgment seat of Christ" (2 Cor. 5:10 in the NKJV).

The judgment seat of Christ is also called 'the bema seat', the place where the Greek participants of the Olympics went to get their rewards. So also we go to this judgment not to receive condemnation (Rom. 8:1), but to receive our rewards for a job that is "well done" (Matt. 25:21 in the NKJV). This does include, however, the fact that we might experience the loss of rewards that we could have had if we would have lived a life that was more in accordance with God's will for us (1 Cor. 3:9-15; Rom. 14:10-13).

B. The Resurrection and Judgment for "Righteous Old Testament Saints":

There is a judgment in conjunction with the resurrection that is found in Daniel 12:1f to verse 3. It is also not for the purpose of condemnation, because these are saved people.[9] But it is for the purpose of giving rewards to everyone who died righteously from the first through fifth dispensations. This is so they will be ready for the Millennium.

In addition, this resurrection and judgment is also for those who will be saved during the Tribulation Period. This is why it takes place after the Tribulation and before the Millennium starts.

C. The Resurrection and Judgment for the Unsaved of All Ages:

The judgment that the unsaved of all ages encounter is called 'the great white throne judgment' (Rev. 20:11-13). It is also known as the "second death" (Rev. 20:5,6 in the NKJV) and is when everybody who has not accepted Jesus Christ as their personal savior throughout all of the dispensations are put into the lake of fire for

---

[9] Ephesians 4:8-10 is speaking of when Jesus Christ went to "Abraham's bosom" (Lk. 16:22 in the NKJV) and brought its inhabitants to Heaven to be with Him. This is why I believe these people will be at this judgment.

   As has been noted, those individuals who are saved during the Tribulation Period will also be at this judgment. They are: 1.) the 144,000 Israelites who are sealed by the Lord in Revelation 7:3-8; 2.) the Gentiles mentioned in Revelation 7:9-14; and 3.) a remnant of Israelites that are found in Revelation 12:6; Zechariah 14:2,5 and Ezekiel 14:21-23.

all of eternity (Rev. 20:14,15; 22:11).[10] It takes place after the millennium and before the New Heaven and the New Earth are created.

VI. The Millennium:

The millennium is the one thousand year period that takes place after the tribulation period and before the New Heaven and the New Earth are created. It is when Jesus Christ reigns in person on king David's throne in Jerusalem (2 Sam. 7:4-17; 1 Chron. 17:4-15; Psa. 89:3,4; Rev. 19:16) with 'born again Christians' at His side on the thrones that He has promised to them (1 Cor. 6:2; Rev. 5:10; 20:4).[11] The Millennium is found in Psalm 72:7-17; Isaiah 2:2-4; Daniel 2:44; Micah 4:1-7; Zechariah 14:16-19; Isaiah 24:23; 34:16 to 35:1-10; Jeremiah 23:5-8; Isaiah 65:19-25; and Revelation 20:4-10.

Everyone who will be saved during the Tribulation, as well as those who will be present at the Daniel 12:1c-3 resurrection, will go into the millennium to start the nations once again.

---

[10] Luke 16:23,24 indicate that people who are in Hades have some sort of a body.

[11] 2 Corinthians 5:8 and 1 Thessalonians 4:17 say that either after death or after the rapture Christians are in the Lord's presence (see footnote #4). This is when we begin to reign with Him (Rev. 5:10), and we live in a 'palace' on earth during the millennium (Song of Solomon 1:4c). As can be seen in Revelation 20:9 (in the NKJV), at the end of the Millennium when Satan is unbound after spending a thousand years in bondage, he "surrounds the camp of the saints". That is speaking of New Jerusalem on earth.

Jewish people, of course, start the nation of Israel (Ezek. 34:11-31), and gentiles start the other nations (Zech. 14:16; Rev. 20:8).

There is only a partial lifting of the Genesis curse during the millennium, because death is still present (Isa. 65:20), and chastening is still necessary (Jer. 23:5). This is why I believe that people who are living on earth during the millennium do so in a resurrection body that was like Jesus' resurrection body (Lk. 24:36-43).

However, the resurrection body is not the final body that everyone will inhabit. At the creation of the New Heaven and New Earth everyone who has not perished in judgment will inherit another perfect body which we will call 'a glorified spiritual body' (1 Jn. 3:2; 1 Cor. 15:42-44; Phil. 3:21).

There is an apostasy at the end of the Millennium when Satan is released for a little while (Rev. 20:7-9). It is for the purpose of testing those individuals that have been born during this time but only have a nominal profession and allegiance to our Lord. In other words, they have not been 'born again' to a heart belief in Jesus Christ. He has given them the chance to 'live for Him' but in their hearts they have not really accepted him as Lord (Matt. 7:21-23).

Needless to say, fire comes down from heaven and devours all those who participate in this rebellion (Rev. 20:9c), so these individuals will be found at the Great White Throne Judgment.

VII. The Final State:

Eternity future is when a New Heaven and a New Earth are created (Rev. 21:1) and is when all the curses, including the curse of death, are finally and for all time done away with (Rev. 21:4).

It comes after the millennium is completed and after our present Heaven and earth are destroyed (2 Pet. 3:10-13). It will also be the way things are going to be for all of eternity (Rev. 22:11).

CHAPTER TWO

The Imperial Powers of the Future and the One World Church

There are two main players during the Tribulation Period and they take over the establishments of the world. They are seen in Revelation, chapter thirteen as two distinct beasts.

The first of these two beasts rises "up out of the sea" (13:1 in the NKJV), and the second comes "up out of the earth" (13:11 in the NKJV). Two things that can be seen when studying the texts pertaining to these two beasts is that the beast coming out of the sea has ten horns, and the beast coming out of the earth has two horns.

I. The Beast That Comes Out of the Sea with Ten Horns:

The first beast mentioned in Revelation, chapter thirteen, comes out of the sea and has ten horns. That this beast comes out of the sea is significant, because it portrays the 'sea of nations.' As John F. Walvoord has written,

> The fact that the beast rises out of the sea is taken by many to indicate that he comes from the great mass of humanity, namely the Gentile powers of the world.[12]

Merrill Unger while commenting on Revelation, chapter thirteen, has said about this beast,

> The beast [has a] wicked career, 6–10. He blasphemes God and those who are His, (6). To this end he wars against the saints, (7a) (Dan. 7:21–22; Rev. 11:7, 12). He is permitted unrestrained power over all earth dwellers except over the elect, (8–10) (c.f. Mt. 24:13, 22). He is the antichrist, the man of sin (2 Thess. 2:3–12; 1 Jn. 2:22, 4:3).[13]

The book of Daniel is a parallel book to the book of Revelation. So this beast is also found in Daniel 11:36-39 where he is militarily inclined among other things.

The horns of this beast are ten 'kings' that give their power to the beast (Rev. 17:12). This beast is the anti-Christ, who has the whole world in his grip (Rev. 13:3,4).

---

[12] John F. Walvoord, *The Revelation of Jesus Christ (A Commentary by John F. Walvoord)* (Chicago. IL: Moody Press, 1974), 198.

[13] Merrill F. Unger, *Unger's Bible Handbook* (Chicago, IL: Moody Press, 1967), 863.

II. The Beast That Comes Out of the Earth with Two Horns:

The second beast in Revelation, chapter thirteen, has two horns and comes out of the earth. This depicts false religion, that from ancient times to the present, has always worshipped the creation more than the Creator (Rom. 1:25). So it is actually the earth that is being worshipped, hence, this beast comes up out of the earth.

Walvoord writes:

> The reference to the second beast as coming out of the earth indicates that this character, who is later described as a false prophet (Rev. 19:20), is a creature of earth rather than heaven... He is pictured [here] as having two horns like a lamb and as speaking like a dragon. The description of him as a lamb seems to indicate that he has a religious character, a conclusion supported by his being named a prophet. His speaking as a dragon indicates that he is motivated by the power of Satan who is 'the dragon.'[14]

This second beast also causes the whole earth to worship the first beast by doing miraculous things (Rev. 13:12–15).[15] This being the case, he is the international False Prophet of the end times.

---

[14] Walvoord, op. cit., 205.
[15] In Rev. 13:12 this beast is almost as powerful as the first beast. However, he only causes everyone to worship the first beast.

Dennis Mather

It could also be that the two horns of this beast are the two facets of false religion of the future - Christian and non-Christian. This is how he is able to encompass the whole earth with a false spiritual power. He includes everybody (This is also portrayed in Revelation 17:15).

III. Two Other Ways of Describing the Two Beasts:

In Revelation 17:3, there is a woman called "Mystery: Babylon the Great, the Mother of Harlots and of the Abominations of the Earth."[16] She is sitting on "a Bright Red Beast Covered with Insulting Names".[17]

The two individuals in this verse will be seen to be as follows:

A. The Bright Red Beast Covered with Insulting Names:

Because this beast is constantly blaspheming God, He has named him "Covered with Insulting Names."

Concerning this beast, Daniel 11:36 says,

Then the king shall do according to his own will: he shall exalt and magnify himself

---

[16] The title of this beast is portrayed in The New King James Version of the Bible, (Nashville: Thomas Nelson Publishers, 1992).

[17] The title of this beast is portrayed in *God's Word: Today's Bible Translation that Says What It Means* (Orange Park, Fla.: God's Word to the Nations Bible Society, 1995).

above every god, shall speak blasphemies against the God of gods, and shall prosper till the wrath has been accomplished.

Since this is the case, the bright red beast is the Antichrist.

B. Mystery Babylon, also Known as a Harlot:

While commenting on Revelation 17:1–12, the *Wycliffe Bible Commentary* says that Babylon is,

> . . . [a] vast spiritual system that persecutes the saints of God, betraying that to which she was called. She enters into relations with the governments of this earth, and for a while rules them. I think the closest we can come to an identification is to understand this harlot as symbolic of a vast spiritual power arising at the end of the age which enters into a league with the world and compromises with the worldly forces. Instead of being spiritually true she is spiritually false, and thus exercises an evil influence in the name of religion.[18]

Again, this is a description of the False Prophet and the worldwide false religion over which he has control. The harlot rules for a while, but as we see

---

[18]   *The Wycliffe Bible Commentary,* op. cit., 1517.

in Revelation 17:16–17, she is destroyed by the ten horns. Then the red-colored beast rules alone.

C. Summary of the Two Beasts:

We have seen the beast that comes out of the sea has been named "a bright red beast covered with insulting names" and is the anti-Christ. And we have seen the beast that comes from the earth has been named a "harlot" and is the false- Prophet. We have also seen the Antichrist as a person who totally hates God and has the whole world under his control (Rev. 13:3). Likewise, we see the false-Prophet as having control of the one-world religious system during the tribulation period and extols the anti-Christ.

CHAPTER THREE

How the One World Government comes about and How It Turns into the Anti-Christ's Evil Empire

To understand how the one world government comes about and how it turns into the anti-Christ's evil empire we must examine two dreams in the book of Daniel. Nebuchadnezzar dreamed the first one, found in Daniel 2:31–35, and Daniel dreamed the second one told in Daniel 7:2–14.

I. Nebuchadnezzar's Dream:

Daniel 2: 31–35 tells of Nebuchadnezzar's dream, as does verses 36 to 45 give the interpretation of the dream. It is about a statue with a head of gold, chest and arms of silver, stomach and thighs of bronze, legs of iron, and feet partly of iron and partly of clay. He also dreamed that "the God of heaven will set up a kingdom which shall never be destroyed" (NKJV) in verses 44 and 45. This latter is the 'kingdom of God' that belongs to Jesus Christ (Zech. 2:10,11; Rev. 20:2-5).

Daniel 2:38 says the head of gold is Nebuchadnezzar. So this part of the statue refers to ancient Babylon, of which Nebuchadnezzar was king. Verse 39 speaks of "another kingdom," arising after Nebuchadnezzar. This would be the silver part of the statue. Daniel 2:39 also speaks of a "third kingdom of bronze," and verse 40 describes the fourth kingdom as being "strong as iron." (These descriptions are all from the NKJV.)

But in Daniel 2:34, 35, as well as in 2:44, 45, the stone "cut out of the mountain without hands" (NKJV), which struck the image on its feet of iron and clay, and broke them in pieces is speaking of Jesus Christ. And as we will see, it is also He who destroys the fourth beast of Daniel's dream in the future.

II. Daniel's Dream:

Daniel's dream, told in Daniel 7:2–14, had four beasts in it. Daniel 7:3 says, "And four great beasts came up from the sea, each different from the other." (NKJV)

As you will notice, these beasts come out of the sea as did the first beast of Revelation, chapter thirteen.

The first beast is found in Daniel 7:4:

> "The first was like a lion and had eagle's wings. I watched till its wings were plucked off; and it was lifted up from the earth, and made to stand on two feet as a man, and a man's heart was given to it." (NKJV)

Stewart C. Easton, in his book *The Western Heritage: From the Earliest Times to the Present,* says that Babylon was like a lion in its dealings with Israel and the takeover of the world,[19] so this beast is ancient Babylon.

Henrietta C. Mears, in her book *What the Bible Is All About,* writes, "The first, or Babylon, was like a lion with eagle's wings."[20]

The second beast is found in Daniel 7:5:

> And suddenly another beast, a second, like a bear. It was raised up on one side, and had three ribs in its mouth between its teeth. And they said thus unto it: 'arise, devour much flesh!' (NKJV)

That this beast is ancient Media-Persia is exemplified by the fact that the three ribs are Media, Babylon[21], and Persia, which was formed about this time by Cyrus, the Median king, after he conquered the other two.[22] Mears says that "Persia was the bear, the cruel animal who delights to kill for the sake of killing."[23] Easton says the

---

[19] Stewart C. Easton, *The Western Heritage: From the Earliest Times to the Present,* 3rd edition (Austin, TX: Holt, Rinehart, & Winston Inc., 1970), 37–44.

[20] Henrietta C. Mears, *What the Bible Is all About* (Ventura, CA.: Gospel Light Publications, 1966), 267.

[21] Babylon was in co-rulership with Media at this time in history (see Easton, op. cit., 44, 53).

[22] Easton, op. cit., 44, 53.

[23] Mears, op. cit., 267.

Media-Persians were gruesome fighters always ready to go to war with their neighbors.[24]

The third beast is described in Daniel 7:6:

> After this I looked, and there was another, like a leopard, which had on its back four wings of a bird. The beast also had four heads, and dominion was given to it. (NKJV)

This beast is ancient Greece which was developed by Alexander the Great. It was given dominion over the whole known world at that time and became greater after his death.[25] Again I quote from Mears:

> "The third [beast] was a leopard or panther, a beast of prey. His four wings portray swiftness. Here we see the rapid marches of Alexander's army and his insatiable love of conquest."[26]

Also, the number four is mentioned twice in the biblical text, which denotes the division of ancient Greece into four parts after Alexander's death at a young age.[27] (We find this also in Daniel 11:4). These four sections each had a governor, which corresponds to the four heads in our text.

---

[24] Easton, op. cit., 45.
[25] Ibid., 101–104.
[26] Mears, op. cit., 267.
[27] Easton, op. cit., 101–104.

The fourth, and last, beast is described in Daniel 7:7. It reads,

> After this I saw in the night visions, and behold, a fourth beast, dreadful and terrible, exceedingly strong. It had huge iron teeth; it was devouring, breaking in pieces, and trampling the residue with its feet. It was different from all the beasts that were before it, and it had ten horns. (NKJV)

This beast is certainly a terrible beast, because the text indicates it devoured and conquered everything in the world, and everything felt its iron rule.[28] Because of these things, this last beast is thought to be ancient Rome.

Mears only says that "The fourth beast was different from all the rest."[29]

One of the reasons this beast is so different is that it has toes of mixed iron and clay. This is portrayed in Daniel 2:40–43.

> And the fourth kingdom shall be strong as iron, inasmuch as iron breaks in pieces, and shatters everything; and like iron that crushes, that kingdom, will break in pieces and crush all the others. Whereas you saw the feet and toes, partly of potter's clay and partly of iron, the kingdom shall be divided; yet the strength of the iron shall

---

[28] Ibid., 118–162.
[29] Mears, op. cit., 268.

be in it, just as you saw the iron mixed with ceramic clay. And as the toes of the feet were partly of iron and partly of clay, so the kingdom shall be partly strong, and partly fragile. As you saw iron mixed with ceramic clay, they will mingle with the seed of men; but they will not adhere one to another, just as iron does not mix with clay. (NKJV)

The significance of this mixture of iron and clay that doesn't adhere to each other pictures how the ancient Roman Empire was loosely held together by its armies.

It also pictures how things have been since the time of the ancient Roman Empire: that many countries now make up the territory that was once occupied by that evil empire.

III. What Is Learned from These two Dreams:

As can be seen, the two dreams parallel each other. They both have four earthly kingdoms: Babylon, Media-Persia, Ancient Greece, and the ancient Roman Empire. And they both tell the story in which the last one is destroyed by Jesus Christ.

However, it is commonly thought the fourth beast turns into the revived Roman Empire of the future (i.e. "deadly wound was healed" in Revelation 13:3 of the NKJV). This means it turns into a one-world government, because it is an all-encompassing world-wide power.

This is found in Revelation 17:9–11:

> Here is the mind which has wisdom: The seven heads are seven mountains on which the woman sits. There are also seven kings. Five have fallen, one is, and the other has not yet come. And when he comes, he must continue a short time. The beast that was, and is not, is himself also the eighth, and is of the seven, and is going to perdition. (NKJV)

But these mountains are not speaking of the city of Rome, or even Jerusalem. Instead, they refer to seven imperialist world governments that have been, or will be on earth since after the scattering of the nations at the tower of Babel.

Commenting on Revelation, chapter 17 John F. Walvoord writes,

> The seven heads of the beast… are said to be symbolic of seven kings described in verse 10. Five of these are said to have fallen, one is in contemporary existence, that is, in John's lifetime, the seventh is yet to come and will be followed by another described as the eighth, which is the beast itself. In the Greek there is no word for "there," thus translated literally, the phrase is, "and are seven kings." The seven heads are best explained as referring to seven kings who represent seven successive forms of the kingdom… [Scripture] does not say, "the seven heads are seven mountains, where the woman sits upon them" and there leave off; but [it] adds immediately, "and they

are seven kings," or personified kingdoms. The mountains, then, are not piles of material rocks and earth at all, but royal or imperial powers.[30]

Revelation 17:10 speaks of the ancient Roman Empire as the sixth of all these encompassing world powers (i.e., "one is"). But the dreams only speak of four of them. The answer to this is that there were two world powers before Babylon. They are: the Egyptian Empire and the Assyrian Empire.

In his book, *Unleashing the Beast*, Perry Stone writes,

> Both past and future biblical prophecy is always linked to Israel and the Jewish people. Of the seven prophetic kings, John, when writing the book of Revelation, indicated that five had already fallen and no longer existed in John's time. These kingdoms began with the Egyptian Empire, which was the first major empire in the Bible to impact the Hebrew people for more than four hundred years (Gen. 15:13). These five kingdoms included: [the Egyptian Empire, the Assyrian Empire, the Babylonian Empire, the Medo-Persian Empire, and the Greek Empire.][31]

However, our text in Revelation 17:9-11 speaks not only of the ancient Roman Empire as the one that was in existence in John's day, (i. e. the sixth empire), but of another one that

---

[30] Walvoord, op. cit., 251–254.
[31] Perry Stone, *Unleashing the Beast* (Lake Mary, FL: Front Line Charisma Media/Charisma House, 2009–2011), 21, 22.

has "not yet come" as the seventh beast. This is speaking of the revival of the Roman Empire.

Leon Wood is another theologian who believes from the evidence presented in the book of Daniel that there will be a revival of the Roman Empire. While commenting on the fourth beast of Daniel 7:8, he writes,

> The correct view [of this] can only be that there will be a time still future when the Roman empire will be restored... a time when ten contemporary kings will rule, among whom another will arise, uprooting three in the process, and then move on to become the head of all... The new horn must symbolize another king, like the others, only emerging later, though while they still rule. Because the description of this ruler, given in this verse and later in verses twenty-four to twenty-six, corresponds to descriptions of the "beast" of Revelation 13:5–8 and 17:11–14, the two are correctly identified. The one so described is commonly and properly called the Antichrist, who will be Satan's counterfeit world ruler, trying to preempt the place of God's true world ruler, Jesus Christ, who will later establish His reign during the millennium.[32]

Not only is the Roman Empire revived (which is a one-world government and is the seventh "mountain" of Revelation 17:9-11), but a strong leader emerges from it to become the

---

[32] Leon Wood, *A Commentary on Daniel* (Grand Rapids, MI: Zondervan, 1973), 187–188.

ruler of the next empire. This is the anti-Christ (Rev. 13:4, 8; 17:11, 12; Dan. 7:20-25). The strong leader's evil empire is the eighth "mountain" of Revelation 17:9-11. Who this is has not yet been revealed, and won't be until after the rapture of the church (2 Thess. 2:8).

CHAPTER FOUR

Other Entities found in the Tribulation Period

We shall study some more entities that factor into this end-time scenario. They are:

I. Edom:

According to Ezekiel, chapters 35, 38, and 39, there is the presence of a strong nation southeast of Israel called Mt. Seir, or Edom. It is the "king of the south" of Daniel, chapter eleven (Dan. 11:5,6,9,11,14,15,25,40).

Of this Unger says, "Mt. Seir is the plateau east of Arabah in which Sela (Petra), the Edomite capital, was located."[33] And Wood says,

> Judging from what exists today, it is noteworthy that Egypt (Ptolemaic power) is still strong and, indeed, the leader of an Arab block of nations.

---

[33] Unger, op. cit., p. 377.

> 'King of the South', then, could well refer to Egypt's principal officer as leader of [a faction of] the Arab world."[34]

However, chapter 35 of the book of Ezekiel says that Mt. Seir, or Edom, is destroyed; and in the context immediately following, (chapters 36 and 37), there is seemingly a peace for Israel.

Unger agrees with this and says, "Chapter 35 is inserted here as a background for chapters 36 and 37, dealing with Israel's restoration to her land."[35] So Israel sometime in the future will have 'peace in the land' after the Arabic nations are destroyed.

It is difficult to know when this takes place. All we are told is that "the whole earth will rejoice" (Ezek 35:14 in the NKJV). when the destruction of Edom takes place. And with the way they like to terrorize, it is not too hard to see how the whole world can rejoice when they are destroyed

II. Magog:

There is another strong nation mentioned in chapters 38 and 39 of the book of Ezekiel. It is called 'Magog' and is from the uttermost northern parts of the world ("far north" in the NKJV). It is thought that it is our modern day Russia.

---

[34] Wood, op. cit., p. 308.
[35] Unger. op. cit., p. 377.

How do we know that "Gog, the land of Magog" is Russia? There are several ways of knowing.

One would be to trace Noahic ancestry to who settled in the northern parts of the earth. For instance, Noahic genealogists generally agree that "Tubal" is the same as the region of 'Tubalsk', and that "Mesheck" is the same as 'Moscow'.

But another reason this is thought to be Russia is that many biblical scholars feel this way. *The Wycliffe Bible Commentary* says of Ezekiel, chapters 38 and 39:

> These chapters describe in apocalyptic manner God's deliverance of His people from an unparalleled invasion by a dreadful foe . . . an invasion previously predicted, (38:17; 39:8), . . . made by nations dwelling in the outskirts of the world."[36].

And Unger says,

> The Great Last-Day Northern Confederacy, 38:1-6: Gog is the leader of the coalition . . . Magog [is] his land. [This is in] the general area [that is] now occupied by Russia ('the uttermost parts of the north').[37]

Magog also has a few allies. They are (as found in Ezek. 38:5,6): 1.) Persia, or Iran; 2.) Ethiopia, or Sudan; 3.) Libya; 4.) Gomer, or Turkey; and 5.) Togarmah, or Georgia and Armenia.

---

[36] Wycliffe, op. cit., p. 755.
[37] Unger, op. cit., p. 378.

Russia's leader, Vladimir Putin, said in 2005 that, "Russia is the most reliable partner of the Islamic world and the most faithful defender of its interests."[38] So it is Russia that invades Israel in the near future.

However, the "king of the north" in Daniel 11:6-9,11,13-15,25 and 40 is not the same person as Gog who is mentioned here. We will see this in the next few paragraphs.

III. Tidings out of the East and the North:

In Daniel 11:44 the anti-Christ hears rumors from the east and the north, and what these two entities plan on doing "troubles" him. This is because he feels it hinders his control of the "whole world".[39]

But who are these people – "the east" and the "north"?

I feel the north here is NATO. The "king of the North" in Daniel, chapter eleven is not the same as who is being portrayed here. The king of the north is a contemporary[40] of the king of the south and the two are the leaders of the

---

[38] MosNews, December 12, 2005. President Putin of Russia said this in the Chechnyian Parliament in Grozny on that day.

[39] With the very highly developed intelligence systems that everyone has in place in our day and age information about another country's affairs is readily available, and I can imagine that the anti-Christ's regime is no exception to this.

[40] Daniel, chapter 11, has both past history and future history. It goes on the premise that history repeats itself when it switches to the future in verse 36.

two factions of the Islamic world – Sunni and Shiite. And in verse 40 it is these two who attack the anti-Christ.

However, here in verse 44, it is NATO that has plans to come against him. I think NATO is going to get stronger, however, the anti-Christ gets wind of its plans and prevails. This is when he occupies Israel - after he has dealt with NATO.

A remnant of devout Jews escapes from him, however, and they "flee to the mountains" (Matt.24:16 in the NKJV).

In Revelation 16:12 the way is made for "kings of the east" to come across the Euphrates river. So it is they who are being referred to as the "east" in verse 44.

It is hard to say who 'the kings of the east' will be in the future, but right now they are, economically, Red China, Japan, and Korea, as well as the Indian peninsula.

And economic power always brings political power, so it could be that these four in the future are the kings of the east.

IV. The United States:

It is generally thought that it is the United States which is one of the entities that is being spoken of in Ezekiel 39:6, because we are included as "those who are living carelessly in the isles" (as portrayed in the KJV). It must be remembered that we are also known as one of the "young lions" of England (Ezek. 38:13 in the NKJV)[41]. However, all we are able to do when Russia and her allies attack Israel is to ask them a stupid question: 'are you invading Israel?' (Ezek. 38:13). But it is good to know we at least have enough resolve at this time to want to know about what Russia is doing to Israel.

V. The Ten Member Conglomeration:

Whenever the phrase 'ten horns' is mentioned in either the book of Daniel or the book of Revelation it refers to the ten member confederation of the last days (Dan. 7:7,24; Rev. 17:12). And this ten member confederation is a revived Roman-like empire. It is also the seventh world empire (Rev. 17:10-11).

I believe this ten member conglomeration is more than just a United Europe and is world-wide in scope. However, a united Europe could be the one who spawns, assembles, and promotes this seventh world power. This is because, it is generally agreed, the "deadly wound" that has been healed in Revelation 13:3 is speaking of the fact that the Roman Empire is 'healed' and revived. The old, ancient Roman Empire's headquarters, of course, was in Rome, which is certainly in Europe. But that is the false Prophet's headquarters. Could he be working out of the World Economic Forum's headquarters in Switzerland? It is near Rome.

---

[41] England has for its mascot a lion. The United States was originally one of the United Kingdom's "young lions."

Also, another reason I think the ten member conglomeration is more world wide than just a United Europe is that the European Common Market right now has more than ten members. So rather than a ten member European bloc of nations, the seventh 'one world power' is a united community of the earth that has ten members.

So I believe Europe will be working more in concert with the United Nations and NATO in the future, with the United Nations becoming stronger every day as the policeman of the world. (Many people think this should be the case, because, they think, "why should America be the one to do it all?")

VI. The Three Super powers:

Three super powers must be conquered by the anti-Christ before he takes over the ten member conglomeration (Dan 7:8,24)

And just as super powers are right now the United States, Japan, and Red China, they could in the future still be these three.

It must be remembered that the Soviet Union at one time was a super power, but right now it does not exist, except as a weakened Russia. Russia will again be strong in the future, but then it will be defeated again during the Magog war (see Ezek. Chapters 38 and 39:1-16). So things can change very quickly.

VII. A United World:

It is evident from what we have seen that the one-world government of the tribulation period is a ten member conglomeration of nations and is the seventh world power of all history, (as it has also been seen that the anti-Christ's regime is the eighth world power). The world has finally come to the place of having one government. And we see this beginning today with globalization in the forefront.

Our present United Nations that has its headquarters in New York City will be in concert with a European union that is in alliance with NATO in the future. The three merge and become strong. They then create the ten member conglomeration by bringing in everybody else.

VIII. The Anti-Christ, and the Eighth Regime:

We have seen that the one world government of the future is the seventh empire to rule the whole world in all of history, and is a ten member worldwide conglomeration of nations.

I also believe the anti-Christ is someone who will be influential in the ten member confederation, and then takes over leadership of it (Dan. 7:8,20-24; 8:9-12,23; Rev. 17:13). But after he takes over the seventh power, he sets up his own regime (Rev. 17:11,12) as the eighth regime, (and the worst ever, I must say).

The anti-Christ also has the full support of the inhabitants of the world (Rev. 13:3c) after he takes over. And one of the ways he does this is to establish a one-world economic system as depicted in Revelation 13:16-18. But the horror of this is that it is the false-prophet that is in charge of this world wide economic system (Rev. 13:12,16,17).

IX. The Three Babylons:

There are three Babylons that can be seen in scripture. The first one is in Genesis, chapter 11, where mankind tried to build a society that would 'reach unto the heavens' (v. 4), but in actuality was an affront to God (v. 6).

The second Babylon, of course, was Nebuchadnezzar's Babylon.

The third Babylon, then, is the hypothetical one that we have already mentioned, seen in Revelation, chapters 17 and 18. It is not a literal city of Babylon, but is typical of the economic power on the earth that is already in existence (2 Thess. 2:7a; Rev. 18:3a). This power is greatly expanded during the tribulation period (Rev. 18:16,-20).

The one-world government has this power riding on its back as a false spiritual power until that evil partnership is destroyed by the anti-Christ (he gives his ten co-horts authority to do this). This is when the anti-Christ thinks he has it all.

But there are events that take place that prove this is not true. They culminate in the Second Coming of Jesus Christ.

CHAPTER FIVE

Some of the Events of the Tribulation Period

There are events of the tribulation period that are chronicled both in Daniel 11:36-12:1 and the book of Revelation, chapters, six to nineteen, as well as throughout the Minor Prophets. For example:

I. The Anti-Christ is Revealed:

The first thing that happens, of course, is the rapture (Rev. 4:1,2), and after this the tribulation period starts. This is when the anti-Christ is revealed, as it says in 2 Thessalonians 2:7,8 and corresponds with Revelation 6:2 where the anti-Christ is depicted as a horseman riding on a white horse.

He is also depicted in Daniel 11:21 as someone who comes into power by 'intrigue', and in verse 23 as someone who has control of a 'small' oligarchy.[42]

---

[42] As has been mentioned, everything that is said before verse 36 of Daniel, chapter 11 is historical in nature, describing people like

II. A Covenant is Made With Israel:

Daniel 9:27 tells of a "covenant" that is made between Israel and the anti-Christ, with the leader of Israel being called "the prince of the covenant" in Daniel 11:22. So I feel this guy is a renegade Canaanite (Ge. 9:25,26) posing as a Jew, which is how he hoodwinks Israel into signing a peace pact with the anti-Christ.

Israel thinks this peace treaty is necessary because of the war they just had to engage in with Russia. This is why I feel the Magog war is very soon after the revealing of the anti-Christ, because the peace treaty is enacted as a seven year 'covenant' (Dan. 9:27)[43].

III. The Covenant Desecrated by the Abomination of Desolation:

The covenant that has been made between Israel and the anti-Christ is broken in the middle of the tribulation (Dan. 9:27;

Antiochus Epiphanies. He is a type of the anti-Christ, because he also desecrated the temple at Jerusalem.

However, beginning with verse 36 it switches to the eschatological future, because this is the first time the term "king" is given to an individual in this passage without it being either the king of the north or the king of the south.

This means that certain despotic rulers such as Antiochus Epiphanies that are found prior to verse 36 are types of the anti-Christ. In other words, Satan has an agenda that he constantly repeats over and over in history.

[43] Weeks in eschatology are actually years and Daniel 9:25-27 must be interpreted according to this fact.

11:31). (I believe the things that Antiochus Epiphanies did from verses 21 to 35 will be repeated by the anti-Christ. If not, why include the account of him doing these things into scripture.)

IV. The Occupation of Israel:

The occupation of Israel is seen in Daniel 8:11-14, as well as in Daniel 11:41 and 45. This begins in the first part of the tribulation period with those who find God's favor being hidden "in the wilderness" (Rev. 12:6,14).

V. The Events Associated With the Four Horsemen of Revelation, Chapter Six:

The four horsemen mentioned in Revelation 6:2-8 allegorically represent events that happen during the entire tribulation period.

For example, the white horseman represents the anti-Christ, because even though he looks like a savior of man-kind, he is in actuality a deceiver. This is because although he appears to be for peace (Dan 11:21,24,27,28), he is actually for war.

Likewise, the red horse represents the wars that the anti-Christ brings with him.

The black horse is the famine that war always brings with it.

And it is also generally thought that the pale horse is widespread pestilence.

So, as it can be seen from these representative figures, the tribulation period is not a period of time that is good for man or beast.

VI. The Two Halves of the Tribulation:

Dan 9:27a, b, c speak of things that the anti-Christ does in the first half of the tribulation period. (See also Daniel 7:25 for a portrayal of the first half of the Tribulation.) Likewise, Daniel 9:27d & e, speak of things that happen in the second half of the tribulation.

That the second half of the tribulation is a horrible time for mankind is confirmed in Daniel, chapter 12, verse one, where it says, "and there shall be a time of trouble, such as never was since there was a nation." (This is found in the NKJV.)

Needless to say, things really get tough for mankind during this time in history. Just look at Revelation, chapters eight, nine, and sixteen for a synopsis of this. If fact, it can really be said that this is the "judgment of the gentiles".[44]

VII. The Trumpet and Bowl Judgments:

The trumpet (Rev. 8:6-11:19) and bowl (Rev. 15:1-16:21) judgments are the things that mankind must endure during the second half of the tribulation period, just as chapter six

---

[44] It is judgment for the Gentiles, because a remnant of Israel is hidden away from all this (Rev. 12:6,14).

of the book of revelation is what mankind must endure during the first half.

The trumpets and bowl judgments are like fireworks in that one of them comes out of the other. In other words, the next one comes out from the former in the form of explosions. In fact, the seventh seal (Rev. 8:1-5) is actually the trumpet judgments, and the seventh trumpet (Rev. 11:15-19) is actually the bowl judgments. So they intensify and are a lot like the plagues of Exodus 7:17-12:29.

In the book of Revelation events are in a glorified chronological order. This means they read like a sporting event where you have sportscasters reporting from a box above the playing field, and also ones down on the field reporting from there. So we have events happening on earth being reported as if they were being seen from Heaven, and we have events happening on earth being reported as if they were being seen from the field.

And we have events being reported that are happening both in Heaven and on earth at the same time. For example, the marriage supper of the lamb in Heaven happens at the same time that people are getting their hands and foreheads stamped with the mark of the beast on earth.

VIII. The Euphrates River Dried Up:

Revelation 16:12 tells of the river Euphrates being dried up. Of this, Walvoord says,

> "The purpose of the drying up of the Euphrates is indicated as a preparation for 'the way of the kings of the east'. The passage is best understood as referring to Oriental rulers who will descend upon the Middle East in connection with the final world conflict described a few verses later."[45]

This drying up of the Euphrates is also referred to in Isaiah 11:15,16 and Zechariah 10:11.

But why dry up the Euphrates? Scripture says it is to help "gather" the world to Armageddon by making it easier for the 'Kings of the East' to get to the Middle East (Rev. 16:12-14).

IX. Armageddon:

The battle of Armageddon is found in Daniel 11:45b; Zechariah 12:9; 14:2-5; and Revelation 19:17-19.

Walvoord says while commenting on Revelation 16:16 that,

> . . . It reflects a conflict among the nations themselves in the latter portion of the great tribulation as the world empire so hastily put together begins to disintegrate. The armies of the world contending for honors on the battlefield at the very time of the second coming of Christ do all turn, however, and combine their efforts against Christ and His army

---

[45] Walvoord, op. cit., p. 236.

from heaven when the glory of the second coming appears in the heavens."[46]

It takes place in the valley of Meggido which is located on the border between the Golan Heights and Syria. (The term Armageddon is a transliteration that means, "the battle that takes place in Meggido".)

But it will be seen that after the battle starts Jesus returns. This is when it says in Revelation 19:15, "...out of His mouth goes a sharp sword." (NKJV) Also this is reminiscent of Isaiah 11:4 where it says, "He shall strike the earth with the rod of his mouth, and with the breath of His lips He shall slay the wicked." (As seen in the NKJV)

I think all He would really have to say is, "Stop!" And this battle would end.

---

[46] Ibid., p. 237.

CHAPTER SIX

The Second Coming of Jesus Christ and the Establishing of the Millennium

We have seen that when Jesus Christ comes back the second time (Rev. 19:11-21), all He has to do is start speaking and that great war called Armageddon crumbles.

It is at this time that the anti-Christ and the false prophet are captured and put into the lake of fire, as also Satan is bound for a thousand years (Rev. 20:1).

Some other events that take place in the Millennium (Rev. 20:1-15) are:

I.   Jesus Christ sits as king on David's throne ruling over Israel in fulfillment of the Davidic covenant (II Sam. 7:4-17; I Chron. 17:4-15; Psa. 89:3,4; Rev. 19:16). This is portrayed at Christmas-time with its heavy depiction of "The King is born" and Jesus as "King of Kings."

II. The Bride is sitting on thrones ruling over Israel with her husband, Jesus Christ (Rev. 20:4). Aren't you glad the Church is the 'Bride of Christ' (Rev. 21:2,9; 22:17)?

III. Israel is living in total peace within her land (Ezek. 34:24-31). Some of the Genesis curses are also removed at this time (Ezek. 36:35; Isa. 11:6-9).

IV. Satan is loosed at the end of the Millennium to again gather the world together to do battle with God's people again (Rev. 20:3,7-9). But, as can be seen, he is not successful this time either (Rev. 20:10).

V. Death and Hades are thrown into the lake of fire (Rev. 20:14,15), as are everyone not written in the Book of Life.[47] This means everyone who was at the Great White Throne Judgment (Rev. 20:11-13), is thrown into the lake of fire.

---

[47] In the Old Testament unsaved individuals went to Sheol (Hab. 2:5) and in the New Testament they go to Hades (Lk. 16:23). The Scofield Bible says these are the same place.

CHAPTER SEVEN

The Future for Christians

After the rapture we're going to be living in New Jerusalem with Jesus Christ for all of eternity (Rev. 20:4). And I think we are going to be oblivious to everything taking place on earth during the Great Tribulation.

However, this is not true of the Millennium, because, as has been mentioned (See chapter one, section VI and footnote 11), we will be living in New Jerusalem. At some time in the future, New Jerusalem "descends to the earth". This is because, Revelation 3:12 and 21:2 say that New Jerusalem comes "down from God". There are those who advocate that it is in the form of a ladder. But Revelation 21:2 seems to say that she was in Heaven and then is transferred to earth.

Revelation 21:18b to 22:5 (in the ISV version) gives a description of New Jerusalem. It says,

> . . . The city was made of pure gold, as clear as glass. [19] The foundations of the city wall were decorated with all kinds of gems: The first foundation was jasper, the second sapphire, the third agate, the

fourth emerald, [20] the fifth onyx, the sixth carnelian, the seventh chrysolite, the eighth beryl, the ninth topaz, the tenth chrysoprase, the eleventh jacinth, and the twelfth amethyst. [21] The twelve gates were twelve pearls, and each gate was made of a single pearl. The street of the city was made of pure gold, as clear as glass.

[22] I saw no temple in it, because the Lord God Almighty and the Lamb are its temple. [23] The city doesn't need any sun or moon to give it light, because the glory of God gave it light, and the Lamb was its lamp. [24] The nations will walk in its light, and the kings of the earth will bring their glory into it. [25] Its gates will never be shut by day, because there won't be any night there. [26] People will bring the glory and wealth of the nations into it. [27] Nothing unclean, or anyone who does anything detestable, and no one who tells lies will ever enter it. Only those whose names are written in the Lamb's Book of Life will enter it.

[22:1] Then the angel showed me the river of the water of life, as clear as crystal. It was flowing from the throne of God and the Lamb. [2] Between the street of the city and the river there was the tree of life visible from both sides. It produced twelve kinds of fruit, each month having its own fruit. The leaves of the tree are for the healing of the nations. [3] There will no longer be any curse. The throne of God and the Lamb will be in the city. His servants will worship him [4] and see his face, and his name will be on their foreheads. [5] There will be no more night, and they will not need any light from lamps or the sun because the Lord God will shine on them. They will rule forever and ever.[48]

[48] International Standard Version, (ISV Foundation, Santa Ana, California – 1996 to 2002, in care of Davidson Press, Inc.)

Printed in the United States
By Bookmasters